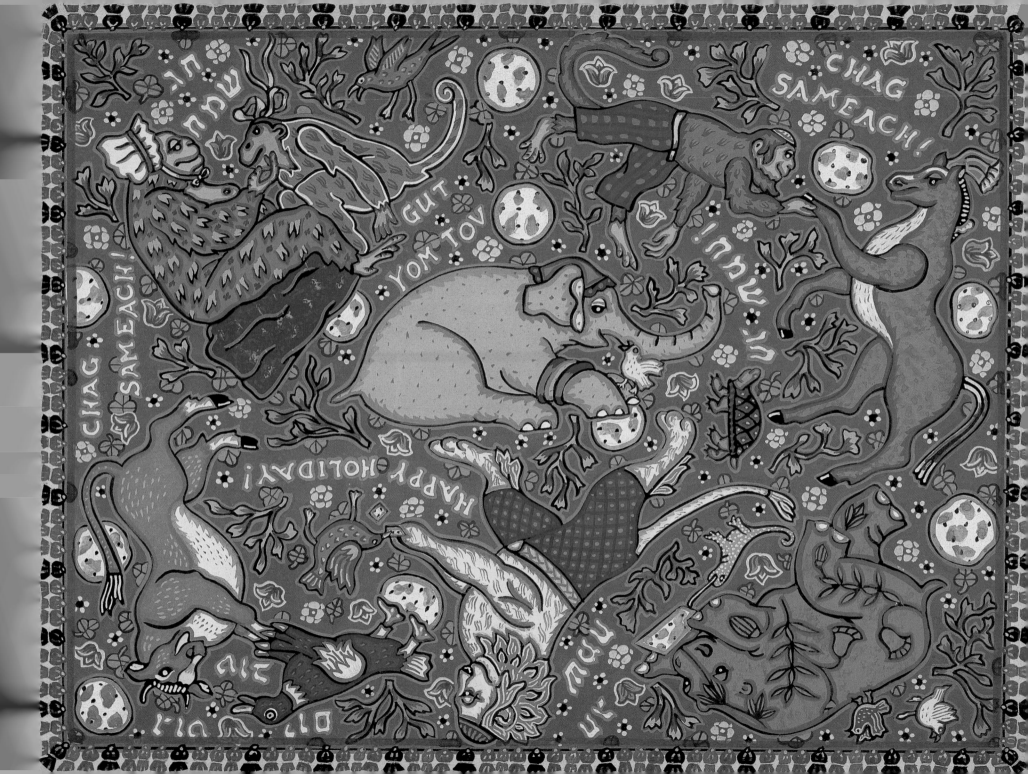

Paintings by ORI SHERMAN

THE FOUR QUESTIONS

Text by Lynne Sharon Schwartz

DIAL BOOKS · New York

Published by Dial Books
A Division of NAL Penguin Inc.
2 Park Avenue · New York, New York 10016

Published simultaneously in Canada by Fitzhenry & Whiteside Limited, Toronto
Text copyright © 1989 by Lynne Sharon Schwartz
Paintings copyright © 1989 by Ori Sherman
Printed in the U.S.A.
Design by Atha Tehon
Calligraphy by Lili Wronker
First Edition
(a)
1 3 5 7 9 10 8 6 4 2

Library of Congress Cataloging in Publication Data
Schwartz, Lynne Sharon.
The four questions/text by Lynne Sharon Schwartz; paintings by Ori Sherman.
p. cm.
Summary: Explores the meaning of Passover by explicating the symbolism of the seder and the four questions.
ISBN 0-8037-0600-6   ISBN 0-8037-0601-4 (lib. bdg.)
1. Passover—Juvenile literature. 2. Seder—Juvenile literature.
[1. Passover. 2. Seder.] I. Sherman, Ori, ill. II. Title.
BM695.P3S385 1989   296.4′37—dc19   88-18881 CIP AC

The art for this book was created using gouache, a painting technique
in which opaque colors are ground in water and mixed with a preparation of gum.
Each painting was then color-separated and reproduced in full color.

To my parents, Earl and Anna Sherman, may they rest in peace,
who made my first seders such beautiful and memorable experiences;
and to my friends Charles Little, Dominic Martello, and Richard Schwarzenberger,
who have enriched my life; and to all my brothers and sisters, both human and animal,
who are not yet free, I dedicate this book.

O. S.

For my nieces, Dara and Jaclyn Sharon

L. S. S.

On a certain night each year when the dark of winter is passing and the world is warming up for the green of spring, Jews in all lands gather to celebrate a joyful holiday. Passover, or Pesach. The house is sparkling clean and everyone is dressed up and the table is set with new dishes and glasses. Everybody has a glass of wine to drink and a book, the Haggadah, with the Passover story and songs.

On the Seder plate in the center of the table are special foods, foods not eaten on ordinary nights. At Seder tables around the world the children ask, What are we celebrating? Why these special foods?

Why is this night different from all other nights?

מַה נִּשְׁתַּנָּה הַלַּיְלָה הַזֶּה מִכָּל הַלֵּילוֹת ?

The mothers and fathers answer: Long ago we were slaves in the land of Egypt. And after years of hard work and bitter sorrow, God led us out of Egypt and set us free. We celebrate to give thanks and to remember how we won our freedom. We do more than remember, though. We tell how it happened and eat the foods and drink the wine so we can feel the story happening to us as it did to the Jews long ago.

Each one of us is free because of what happened in Egypt, and so the Passover Seder is a feast of welcome, of family and friends coming together in gratitude. The door is open. Let all who are hungry come and eat. Let all who are lonely come and join the family. Let all who are curious come and see how we celebrate. And let the prophet Elijah enter and drink a cup of wine too.

The shankbone on the Seder plate reminds us of the lambs the ancient Jews used to offer to God at their spring holiday in hopes of a good harvest.

The roasted egg on the plate means the birth of a new season and a new life. For just as fresh young creatures break out of an egg, the Jews came to life as a nation when God freed them with his strong hand and outstretched arm.

It happened this way.

God chose Moses to go to Pharaoh, the leader of the Egyptians, and say: "It is wrong to keep anyone in slavery. Let my people go."

But Pharaoh refused.

God sent down plagues to frighten the Egyptians so Pharaoh would obey. First he turned the rivers to blood so the fish died and the water was spoiled—no one could drink. He sent thousands of frogs to creep through the land, and then lice to itch, and swarming gnats to torment the people. He sent a sickness that killed all the cattle. He made boils break out on everyone's skin. Hail and lightning destroyed the trees and crops, and locusts ruined whatever growing things were left. And as if that were not enough, God sent a thick darkness that covered the land for three days.

With each plague, Pharaoh promised to free the Jews. But when the plague was over, he went back on his word and said no.

Finally God sent a tenth plague, the worst of all. He sent down the Angel of Death to kill the firstborn son of every Egyptian family.

It was the night of the Jews' spring holiday, when every family sacrificed a lamb to God. Moses told the Jews: "Dip a leafy branch in the lambs' blood and sprinkle a few drops on your doorposts. That way the Angel of Death will recognize you and pass over your houses and not kill your children."

And the Jews did, and the Angel of Death passed over their houses. So our holiday of remembrance is called Passover.

Meanwhile Pharaoh was wakened in the middle of the night by a great cry. When he saw what had happened, when he heard the Egyptians in every house shouting and weeping for their children, he told the Jews: "Go. Your God is too strong for me. Leave Egypt this very night, and be gone by morning."

The Jews packed their things in a tremendous hurry and sped from Egypt, following Moses into the wilderness. God showed the way, leading them with a pillar of cloud by day and a pillar of fire by night.

But back in Egypt, Pharaoh changed his mind again. He sent his army to bring the Jews back and make them slaves once more. The Jews had just reached the shores of the Red Sea when the Egyptian army overtook them. They could not bear to return to slavery. But how could they escape with the sea before them? There seemed no way out.

God told Moses to raise his hand, and as he did, a miraculous thing happened. The waters parted and the Jews passed safely through a path of dry ground in the Red Sea, with high walls of water glistening on either side. When the Egyptian soldiers tried to follow on their horses, the glistening walls of water tumbled over them and they sank to the bottom and drowned.

At last the Jews were safe. In the years they spent in the desert with Moses they learned how to be a community, living with just laws and treasuring freedom.

But, the children still ask, What about the other foods on the Seder plate?

On all other nights we eat either bread or matzoh.
Why tonight do we eat only matzoh?

הַמָּצָה הַזּוֹ עַל שׁוּם מָה:
עַל שׁוּם הַמָּצָה אֵין אָנוּ חָמֵץ וּמַצָּה׃

When Pharaoh ordered the Jews to be gone by morning, they were in such a rush that they couldn't even wait for the dough in the ovens to rise and become bread. They just grabbed the dough and fled.

At the Seder we eat *matzoh,* which is unleavened bread, to taste what our ancestors ate on their flight. Even though it is flat and hard and called "the bread of affliction," or sorrow, we eat it with joy. It is the bread of freedom too.

On all other nights we eat all kinds of herbs.
Why tonight do we eat only bitter herbs?

ūḡ.ḡu ūiu (ēḡu) ūuiu:
Ạēḡ ūḡ.ḡiu ẋri ẋiḡu Ạẋu i.ḡiu'

We eat the bitter herbs because it was so bitter being slaves. The work was long and hard and the masters were cruel. But most bitter of all, we were not our own people—we could not live and work as we pleased. Now our freedom feels more precious as we remember and taste the bitterness where it began.

We eat the bitter herbs along with the *haroses* on the Seder plate—the nuts and apples and wine mixed together. Haroses tastes sweet, like the sweetness of hope, but it looks like the mortar the Jews in Egypt used to make bricks. For that was the work our slave ancestors did, making bricks all day in the hot sun, to build the pyramids and storehouses of the Egyptian cities of Pithom and Raamses.

On all other nights we eat herbs without dipping them into anything. Why tonight do we dip them twice into salt water?

First we dip the greens, which remind us of spring and hope, into salt water to taste the salty tears the slaves shed. For imagine how they must have wept, hating their slavery and wishing for a way to be free.

We dip the herbs a second time to remember the Angel of Death passing over our houses. For, obeying what Moses told them, the Jews in Egypt dipped a leafy branch into the sacrificed lambs' blood and sprinkled it on their doors to keep their children safe from the Angel of Death.

Because Pharaoh was stubborn and refused to free the Jews, many of the Egyptians died of the plagues as well as in the Red Sea. When we drink the wine at the Seder table, we spill some drops to show that our joy is not complete and pure. How can it be, God asks, when so many of his children in both nations died in the struggle for freedom?

On all other nights we eat either sitting up or reclining.
Why tonight do we all recline?

שֶׁבְּכָל הַלֵּילוֹת אָנוּ אוֹכְלִין
בֵּין יוֹשְׁבִין וּבֵין מְסֻבִּין הַלַּיְלָה הַזֶּה כֻּלָּנוּ מְסֻבִּין

When we were slaves in Egypt we worked all day, through years of pain and weariness, with never a moment to rest. We could not do as free people do, which is to work their share and then rest and enjoy themselves as they please. Now we can feast together as free men and women and children, and lean back and eat the good things at the Seder. We recline to show we are no longer slaves. We have no masters, and never will again.

At the Passover Seder we remember that terrible and then wonderful time, and in the remembering, the terror and the wonder happen to us. We were once slaves, now we enjoy freedom. Together we wish that by next year's Seder, all people living in slavery, any place in the world, will pass over to freedom.

· The Order of the Passover Seder ·

1 · Kadesh: Blessings before the meal. 2 · U'rechatz: Washing of the hands.
3 · Karpas: Eating and dipping of a green vegetable. 4 · Yachatz: Breaking
the middle matzoh. 5 · Magid: Asking the four questions and telling the
Passover story. 6 · Rachatz: Washing the hands again. 7 · Motzi matzoh:
Eating the matzoh. 8 · Maror Korech: Eating the bitter herbs with matzoh.
9 · Shulchan Orech: Serving the traditional meal. 10 · Tzafon: Finding
the Afikomen and eating it. 11 · Berach: Saying the blessings after the meal.
12 · Hallel nirtzah: Concluding the service with songs of praise and
thanks to God.